Lance Douglas

This Little Piggy $aved $ome

Snow Canyon Publishing

There once lived five little piggies. Their mother gave each of them ten pennies and she sent them to town for a day of fun.

"Don't spend *all* of your pennies!" their mother shouted as she waved goodbye.

Around the first bend in the road was a wagon full of freshly picked corn. The first little piggy loved corn! He quickly gave the farmer his ten pennies for an armful of delicious corn.

He was so happy!

Soon the little piggies came to a mud hole full of other little piggies playing and having fun. The second little piggy could not help himself. Ten pennies was just what he needed to join his friends in the mud hole.

He was so happy!

MUDHOLE

10 CENTS

When they got to town the third little piggy saw a bright new hat for sale. He loved to wear hats! And ten pennies was just what he needed to buy the new hat.

He was so happy!

The town was full of fun things to do. Ten pennies was exactly what the fourth little piggy needed to ride the Ferris wheel. It was so much fun and........

...he was so happy!

The last little piggy loved corn, and he loved to play in the mud too. He also loved hats, and the Ferris wheel looked like so much fun. But he kept thinking about what his mother had said to them as they were leaving for town, "Don't spend all of your pennies."

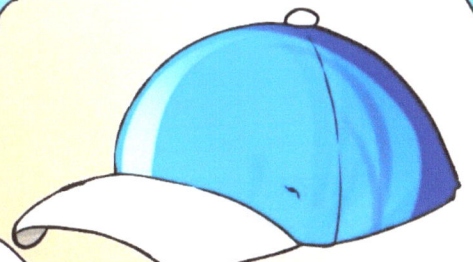

So, the last little piggy bought some corn....but only one.

He loved the mud, but he decided that he could wait until it rained.....

His hat at home was old and worn out, but it fit just right……

And the high Ferris wheel scared him a little.....

It had been a long day. After returning home the five little piggies were very tired. They had so much fun in town! The little piggies fell asleep dreaming about how much fun they had spending their pennies..... except for the last little piggy. He proudly placed the pennies that he had saved into his piggy bank.

Every year their mother would
send the five little piggies to town
for a day of fun. And every year
the last little piggy would add
more pennies to his piggy bank.

Many years later, after the little piggies were grown up, the farmer came to the five little piggies and said, "I am too old to take care of my large corn field. For ten pennies you can buy my entire field. It will provide you with all of the delicious corn you will ever need."

The first four little piggies looked at each other in confusion. They had no pennies left! Each year they had spent every penny their mother had given them.

But each year the last little piggy had saved and saved and saved.
"Sure!" said the last little piggy.
"I would love to buy your beautiful corn field."

.....and he was so happy.

The habit of saving is itself an education; it fosters every virtue, teaches self-denial, cultivates a sense of order, trains to forethought, and therefore broadens the mind.

~ Thornton T. Munger